SURVIVE IN THE WOODS

BY CHRIS BOWMAN

TORQUE ™

TM

Are you ready to take it to the extreme? Torque books thrust you into the action-packed world of sports, vehicles, mystery, and adventure. These books may include dirt, smoke, fire, and chilling tales. **WARNING**: read at your own risk.

This edition first published in 2017 by Bellwether Media, Inc.

No part of this publication may be reproduced in whole or in part without written permission of the publisher. For information regarding permission, write to Bellwether Media, Inc., Attention: Permissions Department, 5357 Penn Avenue South, Minneapolis, MN 55419.

Library of Congress Cataloging-in-Publication Data

Names: Bowman, Chris, 1990- author.
Title: Survive in the Woods / by Chris Bowman.
Description: Minneapolis, MN : Bellwether Media, Inc., 2017. | Series:
   Torque: Survival Zone | Includes bibliographical references and index.
Identifiers: LCCN 2016000306 | ISBN 9781626174474 (hardcover : alk.
paper)
Subjects: LCSH: Wilderness survival–Juvenile literature.
Classification: LCC GV200.5 .B68 2017 | DDC 613.6/9–dc23
LC record available at http://lccn.loc.gov/2016000306

Printed in the United States of America, North Mankato, MN.

TABLE OF CONTENTS

ALONE IN THE WOODS

It is August 23, 2015. Ten-year-old Malachi Bradley is camping with his family in a **remote** part of Utah. He wanders off in search of wild mushrooms.

Malachi soon realizes he has gone too far. He does not know how to get back to camp. He tries to find a road, but has no luck.

"It was weird not having anybody with me, but I just kept going."
-Malachi Bradley

Malachi finds water from a nearby stream. During the night, he curls up between two large rocks. The sun-warmed rocks provide heat and protect him from the wind.

The next day, Malachi hears a helicopter. He knows rescue crews are searching for him, so he stays in a clearing in the woods. Finally, Malachi is found!

"I knew I had to make it back, or my family would be really sad."
-Malachi Bradley

rescue crews return Malachi to his family

LOST!

Hiking in the woods can be fun. But poorly marked trails or bad weather can make it easy to get lost.

If you are lost in the woods, stay in one area. This makes it easier for rescue crews to find you. Keeping a good attitude will help you solve problems until help arrives.

PHONE A FRIEND

It is safer to hike with a buddy than by yourself. Before hitting the trails, always let someone know where you are going and when you will be back.

GEAR CHECKLIST

 fish hooks

 rope

first aid kit

compass

maps

whistle

matches

flashlight

water bottle

 food

 bandana

hat

rain jacket

 bug spray

 knife

FINDING SHELTER

Shelter is important for surviving in the woods. It keeps you warm and protects you from weather. If possible, try to find shelter near a source of water.

RULE OF THREES

You can survive for three hours without shelter and three days without water. You can go three weeks without food.

If you have a tent, set it up on high, flat ground. This protects from flooding. Otherwise, look for a cave or a **hollow** tree. Make sure animals do not already live there.

If there are no natural shelters nearby, build one using branches. Find a low branch or a fallen tree. Lean sticks against the branch or log. Weave in other sticks and leaves to fill holes.

DEAD WEIGHT

Avoid making a shelter underneath a dead tree. Its branches could break off and fall on you.

When you are building, face the entrance away from the wind. A bed of leaves and pine needles can help keep you warm during the night.

MAKING FIRE

A fire can help you keep warm, cook food, and make signals for rescuers. It can also make water clean to drink.

Matches or steel and **flint** are the easiest ways to make flames. Magnifying glasses or binoculars can spark **tinder** using sunlight. Bow drills use **friction** to make fire. A small pile of dry logs and **kindling** help the flames grow.

MAKING A BOW DRILL

MATERIALS: two flat pieces of dry wood, a sturdy stick, a bendy stick (bow), string, tinder

1. Carve a circle into each flat board to fit the ends of the stick
2. Attach the string to each end of the bow
3. Loop the string around the stick
4. Hold the larger flat piece on the ground with your foot
5. Fit the stick into the circle, and keep it upright with the other flat wood piece
6. Spin the stick by moving the bow back and forth until it starts smoking
7. Place tinder near the smoke to help the fire catch

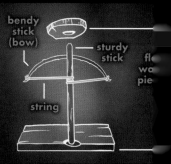

bendy stick (bow)

sturdy stick

fl wo pie

string

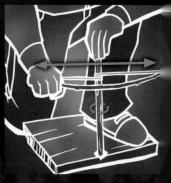

RESCUE SIGNALS

Smoky fires are the best signals during the day. Bright flames are better signals in the dark.

DRINKING AND EATING

Clean water is important for staying healthy in the woods. Water from lakes and streams can be unsafe to drink. Boil it for one minute to kill **bacteria**.

Rain and plant dew are other water sources. If snow or ice is nearby, melt it to make water. Eating it frozen can lower your body temperature.

TREE WATER

Find a non-poisonous tree and tie a plastic bag around a branch with leaves. Keep the bag on for a few hours. Water from the leaves will collect in the bag.

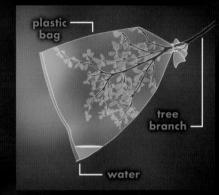

plastic bag

tree branch

water

Forests offer many choices for food. Never eat anything that you cannot **identify**. Many berries can be eaten. But many others are poisonous. Blueberries, raspberries, and blackberries are all easily found and can be eaten.

blueberries

raspberries

blackberries

POISONOUS PLANT FEATURES

mistletoe

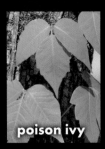
poison ivy

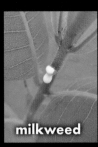
milkweed

- white or yellow berries
- leaves in groups of three
- milky sap
- thorns

Acorns and nuts are other food options. Dandelions also make a good meal. Grasshoppers, **grubs**, and ants are **edible**, but cook them first.

HANG IT UP

Hang any food you have from a tree branch during the night. This keeps it safe from bears and other animals. They are drawn to the smell.

AVOIDING ANIMALS

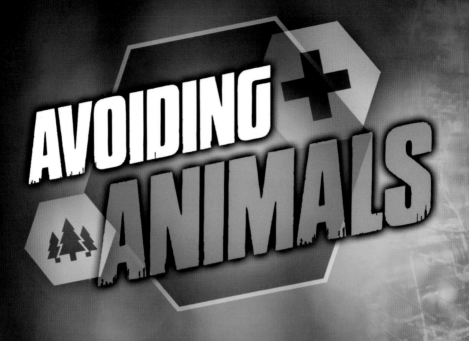

Most animals in the woods do not want to attack you. To avoid scaring an animal into attacking, make noise as you walk. Be aware of what kinds of animals are found in the area.

Always use bug spray and check yourself for ticks often. They can carry disease. Be careful of snakes and spiders in rotting logs. Stay safe until people find you!

deer tick

WHEN ANIMALS ATTACK!

BLACK BEAR
fight back; try to
hit it on the nose
with a stick or rock

MOOSE
back away and talk
softly; if it charges, curl
into a ball and play dead

GRIZZLY BEAR
avoid eye contact and
play dead; spread legs to
make it hard to roll over

MOUNTAIN LION
try to appear bigger and
yell loudly at it; make as
much noise as possible

GLOSSARY

bacteria—small living things that can cause illness

edible—able to be eaten

flint—a hard, gray rock that makes sparks when struck by steel

friction—a force from two things rubbing against one another

grubs—young insects that look like small worms

hollow—empty through the middle

identify—to know what something is

kindling—small twigs or sticks used to start fire

remote—far away from people

tinder—dry grass, bark, or leaves used to start a fire

AT THE LIBRARY

Champion, Neil. *Making Shelter*. Mankato, Minn.: Amicus, 2011.

Kostigen, Thomas. *Extreme Weather: Surviving Tornadoes, Sandstorms, Hailstorms, Blizzards, Hurricanes, and More!* Washington, D.C.: National Geographic, 2014.

Long, Denise. *Survivor Kid: A Practical Guide to Wilderness Survival*. Chicago, Ill.: Chicago Review Press, 2011.

ON THE WEB

Learning more about surviving in the woods is as easy as 1, 2, 3.

1. Go to www.factsurfer.com.

2. Enter "survive in the woods" into the search box.

3. Click the "Surf" button and you will see a list of related web sites.

With factsurfer.com, finding more information is just a click away.

INDEX

The images in this book are reproduced through the courtesy of: Poprotskiy Alexey, front cover (person); Olga Danylenko, front cover (background); Patrick Herrera, pp. 4-5; Ravell Call/ The Deseret News/ AP Images, pp. 6-7; Blend Images/ Alamy, pp. 8-9; SSokolov, pp. 10-11; Piotr Krzeslak, p. 11 (top); Tnymand, p. 11 (bottom); Rafael Ben-Ari/ Alamy, pp. 12-13; studio0411, p. 14; Valentyn Volkov, pp. 14-15; Dave Wheeler, p. 15 (top, bottom); AJ_Watt, p. 16 (left); Valik, p. 16 (right); Maridav, pp. 16-17; D and D Photo Sudbury, p. 18 (top left); Ortodox, p. 18 (top middle); Nitr, p. 18 (top right); Digoarpi, p. 18 (bottom left); Steve Brigman, p. 18 (bottom middle); Christina Leaf, p. 18 (bottom right); robertharding/ SuperStock, pp. 18-19; Aleksei Ruzhin, p. 20; Menno Schaefer, pp. 20-21; KieferPix, p. 21 (hiker).